Rain

on

Me

By Jelyse Williams

Published by: Williams Wordsmith, LLC.

Publisher Address:
Staten Island, NY

ISBN: 978-1-965972-00-7
First Edition

To every Black girl who feels like you're screaming in a void, that your voice isn't heard, that you're at your limit. I see you; I hear you & I love you.

SCAN HERE TO LISTEN TO THE
OFFICIAL RAIN ON ME PLAYLIST

Use this to enhance
your reading experience

Contents

Preface

Rain on Me contains emotionally challenging potentially triggering content that is not suitable for all audiences. Reader's discretion is advised.

As you journey through these pages you will explore the vast complexities of emotions from the point of view of a child maturing into an adult. May these poems resonate with you as you explore the arcs of life.

I
Adolescence

Caution

Caution of what I say and what I do.

Because my feelings are undeniably misunderstood.

All I say, and all I do, can be taken out of place as I read this to you.

I'd say in advance to sit down and relax.

My poems are true and come from nothing but stress due to our world being a mess.

I express my stress the best in words, it makes my emotions come alive, but when I read them aloud,

People's thoughts run wild.

I live quite the life, but when I'm faced with struggle:

I push my emotions to the paper

Just one peep into my life and it gives many people a fright

My words are a visual to situations that were either dramatized or literal

When people can't tell, the results can be quite pitiful.

But I won't waste your time with any more cheesy lines.

Take your time and I'll be your greatest guide,

through the journey of this teenage -> now adult life of mine.

The Caboose

Walk-in. It's your 13th birthday, say "happy birthday"
everyone.
No one does.

They draw a circle on your arm and punch you.
You run away, they chase you, you escape, you're alive.
Like an old train you gasp and wheeze, sputter, and spout,
but still, keep going.

Walk-in, say "hi dad"
he stares.
Hold in all your steam.
Ask if grandpa is ok.

Like a nut rolling off a screw, he replies " he died"
All screws come loose, head searing, steam spouting
everywhere.
Oh, look who came loose
The broken caboose. The broken caboose. The broken
caboose.
Finally, your emotions come loose.

The Painter

This is a new kind of sadness,
A different type of sadness,
A sadness engulfed in a new coat of paint.
A deeper shade of blue.
I want to peel off all those layers and feel anew.
I want a blank canvas...
To start over, but we all know what's true...

You can't start all new, there is still residue.
It's sticky and stiff and I want to do nothing more than RIP
Off the sadness and slap on the joy.
Give it a label, smile bright, like a child with a new toy.
But that residue is stuck to my mind like glue, together like
conjoined twins because my residue says that "we're never
through"

Jamaica

Jamaica, oh Jamaica,
my mother's homeland, a land that's not my own.
A place of beauty and wonders.
A simpler, quieter place.
So rich in culture, love, and creativity.

Jamaica, oh Jamaica,
a beautiful land
a place of wonders and beauty
beauty and wonders...

Jamaica, oh Jamaica,
one day I shall arrive to my mother's homeland.
A land that was never my own.
Oh, a wonderful land I'd like to see.
A wonderful land that never belonged to me...

Jamaica, oh Jamaica.

Headache

I get frequent headaches nowadays.
Sleep in and laze
Because I'm not on my usual craze.
My scribbling pencil sounds like music to my ears and as I
write, the world around me disappears.

Why do I keep getting sudden surges of sadness?
I need it to end.
I just crave a day...
No, a year!
Where I can be happy again.

Oh gosh. Oh jeez. Oh lord.
My head is storming and the pain in this clip has clearly been
forming for a while.
Although I choose to be mild, my thoughts run wild.
Oh my. Oh me. Oh gee.
My head is spinning, and it isn't supposed to be

Disappointment

Clank clunk clink my heart starts to sink.
Splish sploosh splash my heart starts to thrash.
Zip zop zoop there it goes.

Then a crash.

It starts to beat fast.
Chitter chatter, chatter chitter, I start to shiver.
I open my mouth, but can't speak, my eyes can't meet, I'm
mentally beat.
I never want this incident to never repeat.

Rise

I rise. I rise. I rise. I rise.

There is a reason for it all, why they want to see me fall.
Why they don't want me to rise in their blue skies as it brings tears to their eyes.
My rise will bring sunny skies and kiss the world's worries goodbye.
I will bring success in a world that has deemed me a failure.
That thought makes me fly because

I rise. I rise. I rise. I rise.

Confessions

I confessed all of my thoughts, words, and feelings and
whispered them into your ears.
You
took those words and cut me down and
left me to bleed.

Sharp jabs to the chest, a tug of the heart strings.

I've endured all the torment you put me through because I
loved you
Or so I thought.
Each word that slipped off your tongue was a lie.

A penetration to the soul, heart scabbed and bruised.

The man I once knew before illuminated and sparkled is now
worn and broken.
Like an old record player, you keep repeat-eat-eating over and
over again.

Down

I'm down.

It seems like again everything turns my smile into a frown
My frustration looks like anger and my anger looks like
insanity
I even wanted to cut off my crown
The emotions inside me, give me anxiety
I'm down.

I just want to come back around
As my eyes look around it's like I hit rock bottom and I'm
facing the ground
My feelings echo like surround sound
And as I close my eyes and listen

I hear it
What's keeping me earth-bound
And is making my heart pound
I'm down.
I'M DOWN.
I'M DOWN.

Appearances

Look at me.
Look at her.
She's not me.
I'm not her.
She has curves, that's superb.
She's smaller, I'm taller.
I have brown eyes, hers are hazel.

My shape and size do not define my human mind
And even if someone was a copy of me, they wouldn't be me
because I am so intricate,
So fine, that your human minds can't repeat another one of
my kind.

And so are you

You are so detailed, so perfectly imperfect that no other
human that comes to mind will ever be that fine.

II

Transition

Battle

I was wrong wishing to be right.
I'm a hypocrite.
Giving advice that I'm too scared to follow
I keep my lips zipped tight instead of fighting my own fight.

The fear of how I'd react keeps me humble and earthbound
But when will I stop bouncing around?
When will I fight my fight and turn my wrong into a right?

Jab. Kick. Duck. Twist.
An endless battle that I think will forever last
But are only a few seconds for those who've looked past.

Hook. Cross. Slip. Cross.
I'm fighting with an iron hook, and I don't care who's going to look.
I'm going to right my wrong and end this battle strong.

Clouded

Head clouded with thoughts unimaginable.
Frustration takes over and makes me feel worse.
Push it to the back of my mind and distract myself so they won't see
That there is something fascinating, frustrating and furiously going on with me.

Head clouded, mind filled with doubts and
The situations at school makes me want to shout
While I try to keep my cool, people play me as a fool.

Head clouded, as my friends sputter and spout and I see their true colors,
What they're really all about.
I think of the ones I thought I could trust in.
It brings more clouds, grey and crowded.
I want to break out,
Head clouded.

Summer Sun

The clouds clear as the sun makes its way through.
A strong glow that provides no heat
That's the sun in the winter, man it's got me beat.

This year... no this decade and many decades going forward.
I want to be the summer sun!
The one that glows and ignites a golden flame that heats the
sand under people's toes.

A summer sun, whose heat no one can compete
A summer sun, whose shine brings joy on the rise

I'm tired of being the winter sun whose shine make people
blind
Who's only there just for show.
And disappears right before you know.
I want to glow and shine and bring joy on my rise
Because my shine affects other people's lives.

Shower Thoughts

How do I give advice that I don't receive?
Lord, I do that more times than others may believe.

Self-love is essential to being able to truly know and help
yourself
While my own love is what I received, my confidence is what
needs to pick up the same speed.

Face? beautiful but boxy.
Thighs? Strong but thick and when I look at them, I feel
nothing but sick
Body? A work in progress, but when will it be completed?
My impossible standards block the love that I breathe,
through my lungs it turns into a wheeze,

My blocked passage makes it hard to find a sound connection
between my heart and mind
But one day I'd be inclined
To push my confidence to the same line as the love
surrounding my body, soul, and mind.

Message To

This is a message to momma:

As my tears flow, I don't know which way I must go, as the pain in my heart only seems to grow, and I know that you have work of your own, but your daughter who is almost grown barely knows how to control the emotions in her soul.

This is a message to papa:

Our relationship seems as cold as the tip of an iceberg in the North Pole, if only I could know how to go through your bold mysterious mask, played as confidence and oh as you dance around the question and question my intelligence, it pushes me farther away and makes me want to keep it that way.

This is a message to my sisters:

I love you both with all my heart and I'm sorry that we are always apart, my hurt and pain made me push you away, but all you wanted was a sister who you could play with all day. I feel like a stranger to you and that you don't know me like I want you to, and I hope I can do what's good for you and truly hear you two like I'm supposed to do.

This is a message to you.

Fake Friends

I'm for the movement but against the people who rule it.
Like a package sent through the mail
I'm kicked and ripped by people who don't care.

And when I receive a tear, it seems like my "supporters" don't
seem to be anywhere.
When I scream and yelp, none of them come to my help.

I tumble and turn and fix myself up and then,
They start to the crowd

Oh, now they turn up again.

Treat me like a burden, I'll treat you like a ghost
And ignore you when you need me most.

Free

I used to wish to be normal and take away the memories that
pained me,
But those are the memories that shaped me and then I truly
"Became me"
I wished to be the old me, the me that felt free.

I didn't think about the limits of life and money
Things caused me no strife.
My parents didn't argue.
I didn't care about my body.
I didn't have to think about becoming an adult.
I barely felt lowly and lonely.
I didn't see the color of my skin or care about the one's others
were in.

I speak for myself, and I speak the truth:
I want to live
Happily. Healthily. Lovingly.
These memories haven't made me. They've shaken me.
But I pray that one day I'll finally be okay.
And that instead of shaking me, it'll cause me to become free.

Lost

I wept inside as the fear of my eternal tears will bring stares
And oh-
How life is unfair...

But who am I to judge when I did the crime?
When you can see my thoughts covered in dirt and grime.
I'm the one who has caused myself, my own hurt.

Procrastination for my lack of motivation.
My coping mechanism... my shell is falling through, poking
me, stabbing me, it went so far in that I don't feel it anymore.
People always say *"Why don't you stop your pain right away?*
Don't you know that this doesn't hurt me, but you?"

As I gaze away, I start feeling the tiniest pain and a message
keeps panging in my membrane,
The same one that always beats in my brain:

"Why don't you take the pain away, stop heading astray, you
know that you've gotta face your feelings someday."

Rain on Me

No Name

I feel weighted, absolutely down and I hate it, dealing with
these expectations of my family and myself, wondering when
I can finally feel as if I made it.
My smallest accomplishments feel like nothing and when I
think of my past, sometimes it feels as if I can't escape it.
6 years. 6 years of endless tears. 6 years. 6 years of endless
turmoil and fears. 6 years. 6 years and now I'm finally near the
end of my childhood.

Many are from the outside looking in.
I used to fear others counting out my sins
Like it's judgment day and I used to pray that one day
My cheery facade and my beautiful bonds and amazing grades
wouldn't break,
And that these slip-ups and failures and makeups could only
be seen by God.

It's stressful as a black girl, in a world where you are looked
down upon.
It's stressful as the oldest acting as the strongest and boldest,
for my little siblings to see.
It's stressful as a daughter of an immigrant mom, now U.S.
citizen, to pick up the slack and break up the chains of the
past where our only path is to let ourselves lose and others
win.

To drown & sink in our sorrows & not live to see tomorrow.
To make us rot & now live on our blocks, to push us to the
curb.
To say that our success wasn't the best just to step on us.
To crush us.
The roses growing through the concrete.
To maintain their power over us so that we may never flower.

I shot for the moon, and I made it.
Everyone saw me do it, there's no way you could fake it.
More & more people want to make it to the moon, so they try
to pull, push, and prod to make it there, without seeing the
trials that made me make it.
6 years. 6 years went straight down to the pavement. 6 years. 6
years. 6 years. They don't see what made me make it.
6 years. 6 years. 6 years? And they still don't know where I'm
gonna go, they just wanna pull me down because they can't
take it.

But then I realized I'm not no goddamn spaceship.
Put in the work, try to succeed.
I can give you the recipe, but you are the chef that you need.
I made it to the moon now I'm coming for Mars.
It's you that needs to set your standards, set your own bars.
I'd like to see you succeed without putting me down, put
yourself together, and grab your own crown.

My struggles are not me, but they've led me to succeed and
taught me that God, my family, my friends, and sometimes

even teachers are the ones for me.

I may go down the wrong way today, but I got them and myself to lead the way.

I know that my story isn't through & that my legacy will be huge and hopefully will impact you too.

III

Love & Loss

Lovergirl Laments

----------------message to him -----------------
As I stare into space, I can't believe my feelings got in the way
of my success again
You're a friend's dream and a lover's nightmare
You make me smile but you make me want to scream
I thought we went over this
When can I be free?

Lovergirl for life so
Even if my mind gave up and is made up
My heart is still going to fight

Trifling truly stifling
My feelings make it hard to breathe around you
I feel trapped at sea, stuck in a wave of emotions and even
when I feel like the tides are low, just like that
A conversation or being around you sends another wave
straight at me

A total wipeout, can you truly not hear my heart cry out?
For you, I would put myself on the line but I'm tired
Of the unreciprocated yet somewhat requited feelings
Enough is enough I know that it's tough but the lock you
have on me has to be released

Free bird caged by her own feelings.
Oh, I missed just being me and I'm happy you came into my life but why did I have to like you?
Why did I have to feel for you as more than just a friend?
I wasn't even on that type of timing...
But as I got to know you my defenses went down, I found someone who could truly feel me, and I could be close to.

Get rid of it, get rid of it, get rid of it
I'm sick of it
Sick of it
Sick of it
I just want to be friends
My feelings are only hurting just me in the end

----------------message to God ----------------
God why? I don't want anymore tests I can't rest without thinking about him
But his mind isn't on me, I'm like option number 3 or 5 or maybe way further down the line
And I know he doesn't mean it but how come he can't see how much this is hurting me

Turn your brain off
Switch it to friends only mode
Even if he mentions others, don't cry! Be there for him. He's there for you, isn't he?
Stop being dramatic: sprinkle some advice in, listen as a friend, don't be selfish he's your best friend in the end

As I flick the switch to turn my feelings off, I feel my heart
breaking into more pieces
As I hear about another hookup or new interest
And encourage him to pursue it because
I already know we can't be together, we talked through it.
But oh, it hurts and feels the worst

Why can't it just disappear
Why can't I just disappear? I want to, but know that I can't
because why would I ever ghost one of the best friendships
I've ever had?
God if this is a test I know that I'm passing but every step of
the way hurts

You're testing my kindness, patience, and communication,
and the last one as I'm getting stronger, I feel my heart
weighing heavier
The conversations I don't want to have is being initiated by
me
I've never thought I'd see the day when I'd be confronting
anybody

My soul is on fire and God you are my number one desire
I beg of you please just take these feelings away
So, I can have no more pain
So, we can go back to normal
Just friends nothing too formal
We'll be close but not too close
Best friends with boundaries

Friends hopefully to the end
I don't want to lose him, but God forbid if I do I know I'll be
fine and so will he because you have great plans for our lives

------------------ in the end --------------------
Here is my lovergirl's lament as I give my two cents on the
situation that I so desperately want to be out of

I'm so proud of myself for getting it out,
for the growth I've done.
Last time I checked I couldn't even write one stanza of a
poem
Hopefully, in the future, I'll cringe at this and grin at my
progress and the future of my life and his life
Hopefully, he has a nice life. His doctorate and a lovely wife

I hope for me I become more positive and get a husband who
loves me for me
One who indulges in what I love to do and loves God as
much as or way more than me
Someone who can pray for me and give me strength as I can
do the same for him

One day....
One day...
One day.

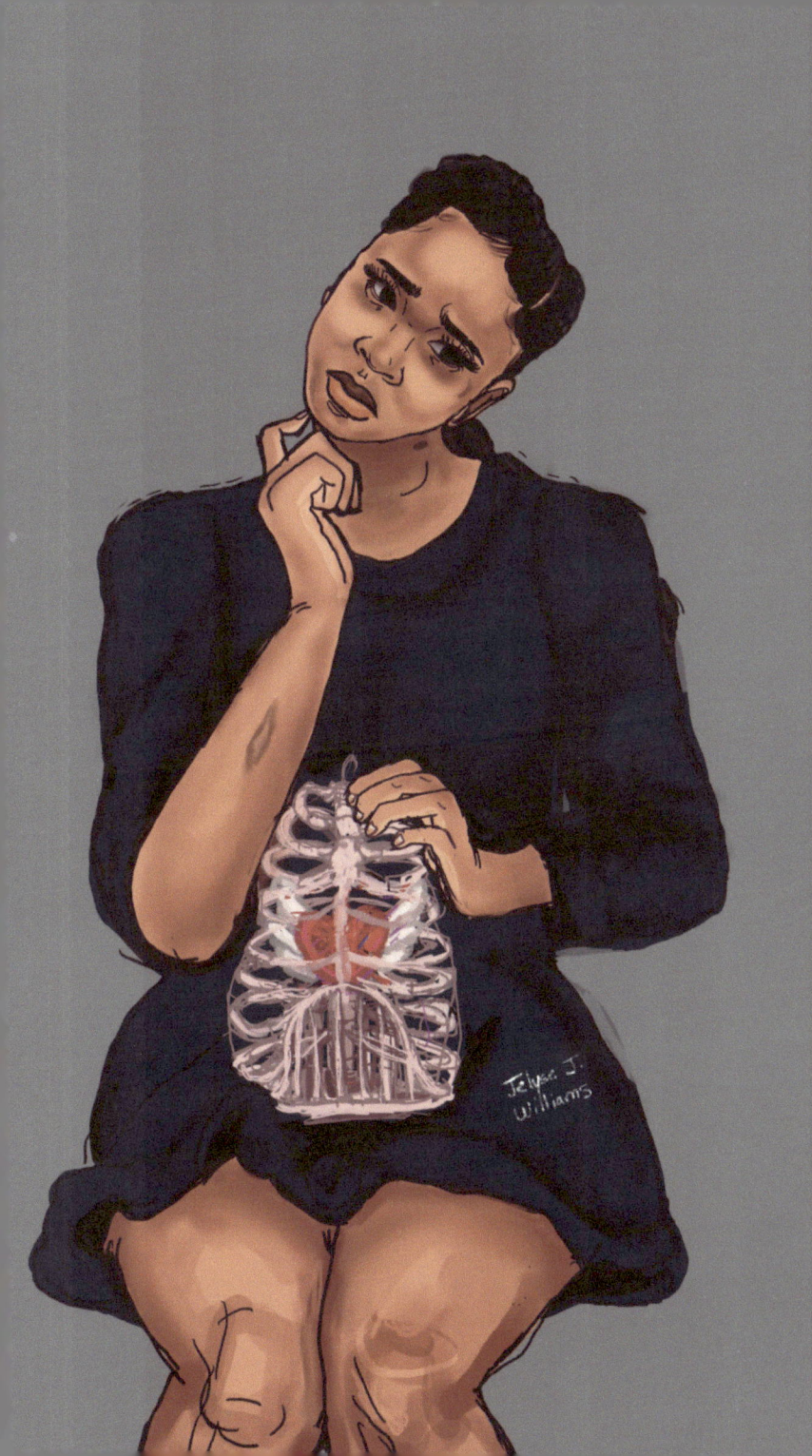

Played

I thought this dude was playing Connect 4,
so, I was playing checkers
when he was really playing chess

I can't do anything but stress the fact that I played myself

He gave me the warnings and the signs, yet I turned a blind
eye

My hopefulness turned into faith and that was my big
mistake

I feel dumb and there's nothing else I can say but
the fact that I relayed so much of my personal life to someone
who sees me as less than a friend
is the worst offense I could make to myself

Was it a cry for help?

Just to get attention?
Was this something that I needed?

My rose-colored glasses made it hard to see anything other
than that pretty-in-pink perfect fantasy that I projected upon
a person who had "potential."

The Haunting Feeling of Falling out of Love

The haunting feeling of falling out of love
I feel the ghost of you touch my heart
The spirit of what could've been, lingering on my mind
Shivering, missing the warmth of your touch and finally fully
understanding the gravity of this situation
What it feels like to not be a priority...
My heart aches because of your vacancy
You moved on oh-so-quickly
Did I even matter to you?
I guess I did... but not in the way I wanted to matter
Who am I kidding, it felt doomed for the start
Like my many endeavors and heartfelt relationships... it will
all come to an end.

Doomed from the Start

Sometimes I ponder the possibility if you could ever die from
heartbreak
If I could ... would that mean you're slowly killing me?
Still picking up the rubble,
the remains of my heart because of all the trouble you've
caused.
I caused...
I guess I did this to myself.
You told me not to love you, but I did. I tried to leave but you
played on my feelings.
Heartbreak ain't a joke, as I choke on the words, I want to say
but can't utter.
I tried
I tried
I tried.
You kept face but at the same time lying, subtly letting me in
Now I doubt the friendship and everything you told me
about

Papier Mâché Heart

My heart was ripped out, transfigured by these never-ending tests.
When can I ever rest?
Putting your heart on your sleeve is the quickest way to bleed
Advantage, take advantage...
Candy, my heart is like candy...free in a basket for the taking,
Snatch each piece, leave all the ugly bits for me.

My First Love

My first love has been lost
At the cost of my heart, I pushed for something that wasn't
there
The death of love...
while he's alive and well
My heart is crushed by the weight of disappointment and
unbearable loneliness

How can I be lonely in a room full of people?
They're all here, but when you used to be near, everyone
around us would disappear
Slowly but surely, I feel us drifting apart
It's all over, but nothing has really begun
How am I feeling heartbreak when we weren't even together?
Maybe this is for the better...
Have a nice life
Sayonara to the person I used to be, you took the remaining
pieces of me.

Because I'm hurt

Note: This is based on the line in Lovergirl Laments where it says, "Why would I ever ghost one of the best friendships I've ever had?"

————————————————————

I can't explain in words how weak I feel...
As I lie in my bed... my body feels heavy, my fingers feel limp,
it feels as if I am falling back to earth
Body trembling,
Mind scribbling,
Stomach coiling and uncoiling,
Emotions unrecognizable and unorganized

I feel like I'm just rotting away...
I have hope for my reality
But my mind is blocking me from the future I desperately
want to see

Is it because we stopped talking?
Is it my fault? Is it me?
I'm just hurt.
I'm hurt and it sucks
I feel like a ball of emotions ready to explode
But I need to keep my facade -
to keep me under control

Smile and wave, it'll be okay...
That's what one part of me likes to say
But on the inside, I feel like everything is on fire
I finally felt happy!
Or was I?

I was happy being around him
But I hated the predicament I was in.
I did my research, and watched videos on dating, but how'd I
end up in this situation?

Were we dating? We weren't but we felt like we were.

"What are we?"
"Are we just friends?"

Those two questions were the beginning to my end...

I opened up too early.
Now I see that I just need to make time for me...

My reaction is quite delayed as I keep replaying the scenes in
my head, it feels as though there's nothing else to be said

You live and you learn
Not everyone is meant to be in your life
But that doesn't make it hurt any less

I told him about my past, my anxiety, my parents, my ideas.

Oh how...Stupid

How

Stupid

How

Stupid

How

Stupid

Linger

Were we dating? We weren't, but we felt like we were.
I can't believe I was in a situationship
I feel robbed of a relationship that I wanted to develop and
work, but
That wasn't the course of our lives

I technically didn't say goodbye to you...
I just don't want to be hurt anymore.
I'm drawn to your warmth but every time I get too close I get
burned.
I'm just protecting myself...
Right?

Prioritizing my health.... Helping me.
So tell me why I feel like the asshole in this?
Why am I torn and feel like I'm hurting someone I love

Every time I see you heart someone else's message and avoid
mine
or avert your eyes away from me
I get a pain in my chest, it feels like I'm a target with an arrow
attached to my heart

We were friends. Best friends. So close that I told you things
that I've never told anybody.
I feel betrayed but should I even feel that way?

A lot of the actions you took rubbed me wrong
I felt like I was vulnerable, with no defense against your
charming yet somewhat calculated advances
Your oh-so-subtle glances at me
The words that you'd say and the actions you made

Do I have a right to feel angry?

This is so illogical

I feel hurt and betrayed and it's a bit hard to look at you the
same
I think you're standing back to give me time to feel what I
need to feel
But I just want you to check on me once.
Ask me how my day was
We can go back and forth and finally, my heart will go back to
feeling weightless

But I'm scared of getting burned again
By someone who I call my best friend.
I don't call many people that, you're 1 out of 2;
even many people I hang out with are close or regular friends.

I feel as though my heart has been ripped out of my chest it
feels hard to breathe.
I'm scared that you're going to leave,
Now I'm preparing myself for the worst

I don't know what your thoughts are going to be if you read this

But I feel angry at you... a bit crossed even,
I hope that what I saw wasn't true, that you still haven't seen her after all the things I told you.
But it's your decision and the only person I can control is me and I can't control what you do.
If it is true I don't know what to say...
I know I told you I was over these feelings
And you were right to hold off certain conversations because emotionally I feel like a wreck
I'm over it mentally but not emotionally
This is the first time I ever felt something like this.
No infatuation felt like this before

I'm done with the weird situationship thing but I still and will always value our friendship

God... if this is your way of character development this is sick...

Burnout

I hate you
I hate you
I hate you
I hate you
I hate you

But I don't really
I just hate how you made me feel
The fact that you're fine
And I'm miserable...
You're not even my ex

We never even dated
Fuck... why am I writing about you so much?
Do you think this is a joke?!

This is so stupid...
I should be enjoying my life right now
I feel like I'm under a curse
I feel like I can't hear God and it's been difficult to pray

I'm in such a slump it's not even funny
I hate feeling like this...
It feels like the real me wants to burst out of this wannabe's
chest

I can't take it anymore I feel like a fake in my own body
Waddling around the earth,
Arriving in places without consciously knowing how I got
there

I feel so dumb, so stupid
I want to scream
I don't care if it makes me look crazy

Why did God make me this way?
I just want to live a normal life!
I have a fucked-up life and a fucked-up head
My brain constantly feels on fire, and I feel no desire to do
what I want anymore
I just feel tired...

I don't want to move
I don't want to feel pain anymore
I just want to sleep

It hurts so fucking much; my chest...
I'm so tired
I'm so tired
I'm so tired

And I can't tell anyone
What would they say?
I don't want to give someone this...

Jesus... just when I felt like I picked up the pieces.
You were helping...
Then it got smashed into smaller ones.
Although I reglued up most of them
The cracks show... and I tried ignoring them, but I can't
anymore

I feel a hole where my heart used to be.
A papier mache body that the rain washes away.
While my heart feels everything, and my brain feels nothing

Everyday it switches, where my brain feels everything and
then my heart feels nothing but empty

Nothing is the same...
I wanted things to be different and I tried my damn hardest

I'm tired of proving myself to people
I'm tired of being everyone's spectacle

Stop watching me!!
Please...

If no one sees me anymore
I can finally disappear...
Slip under the surface
Hopefully no one notices.

hate you'
i hate you
i hate you

Burnout

Jelyse
J. Williams

Oh Really?

After all this time you finally want to talk to me?
I don't know whether to laugh or cry
All I can do is sigh and chuckle
Ha Ha ha Ha
Ha ha ha....
No way.
No
You're not serious
Are you?

You know what's crazy
This whole month and some change while I was crying
When I was in the deepest pits of despair
When I was feeling anguish and needed somebody
...I couldn't talk to anybody...

I will not allow someone to, just come back into my life when
they're bored
Come to me correct or don't come to me at all.
I'm tired of having to explain this to people
Mainly you.
Explain my feelings, when I have countless times
Explain why your actions had me messed up, only to have you
in the end just do the same thing to me again

Yeah, maybe I was coming off too strong
And yeah, maybe my feelings were too intense
But they were real nonetheless

I was attracted to you because I thought you were real
But you unsuccessfully concealed your snake-like nature
I'm not angry anymore just sorry for you
I see a sad boy who uses girls to fill the void in his heart
And I will no longer be one of those girls

I'm decentering men fully
It's time for me and me only
I gotta upgrade myself, because clearly when it comes to it
I see that I'll be left in the dust and will be the only one to
fully pick myself up.

Mental Gymnastics

I don't think I'll ever be the same girl after this
Why do I have to play mental gymnastics and mind Olympics
just to fall in love?
It's so freaking stupid.

Like oh, just because you think that I'm easy to manipulate,
you think that I'll tolerate your bs

But I won't.

My entire being is out of its element.
Soul hardened.
Poked, Prodded, Picked and Stitched.

When I was a girl, I thought my mom and aunt were being
"mean"
I thought that could never be me.
I thought, that if I treated people the way I wanted to be
treated, and gave them all of the love in my heart then I'd
receive the fruits of my labor
Sweet and fresh

But I was naive
Now I see
See that this tree only bears bad fruit
This harvest was rotten
I couldn't use these crops to feed anyone
No less myself.

No matter how many of these seeds I sowed, I'd always reap
the same results with you.

IV

Maturation

The Intersectionality of a Black Woman

My intersectionality has me questioning my reality
As a Black woman looking for support and assistance
but is handed a wall of never-ending persistence of hatred
for her existence from all-skinned folk
Even those that are supposed to be her kinfolk

The world has let me know that I'm black before I am a
woman
The world sits back and relaxes at the sounds of my suffering,
our suffering
Because our pain is their gain.

They say:
"I love Black girls. Their chocolate skin. Lemme get some of
that melanin."
Oh, is that so?
It's sad that black girls look up to this because they're being
exploited for likes and comments that turn into profits going
back into these white boys' wallets.

Constantly ignoring the obvious cues and clues that we leave
showing our hurt.
That is constantly exploited because to them we're just a
trend.
Something to jump on. To step on. To stomp on.

Where were you then?
Where my melanin was just as Poppin. My hair, just as
Luxurious. Features, just as Show-Stopping.
Where were you then?
When my people kept crying out. Our pain, so great that
we would scream and shout. But was ignored by everyone
around us.
We're "dramatic, over-exaggerating, pretending" they'd say.
But where were you when this was happening?
When we were calling out and you were raising your doubts
and hoped this conversation of our struggles would end that
day.
Now the words we spoke are being repeated out of your
mouth as your silly-little agenda pretending to be fake woke.

Constantly forced to conform to your norm because it
doesn't fit your standards
But if it was on a white woman, she would receive no slander.

Give Me a Reason

As I lie back and sigh
I question why I'm in this position again.
Sitting back and wondering the reasons why I should live
As I'm struggling to create the thoughts, the tighter the knot
in my stomach grows

Man...life has me beat, as I try to stand up and face it I fear I
can't take the heat
If I try to take myself out of the kitchen, people will wonder
why I went missing.
They'll blame themselves. Ponder why I didn't ask for help.
I'm not a burden that they see, but how come I feel that way
about me?

Give me a reason to live.... Give me a reason to cry... The
world may cause me harm, but I don't want to say goodbye

Heart to heart connection,
It's time that my mind finally learns this lesson:
Life may be difficult but in any situation, it too shall pass...
Mental scars shall not harden my heart
And while I may wear it on my sleeve, I believe that soon this
lover girl's foundation shall not be shaken.

It's hard to take this lesson when I'm stressin over life, just
wanting things to go right

when so many things are wrong.
Forcing myself to be strong for everyone when I feel like
everything in my life has gone asunder
I feel sick... I know I've made it this far but life wasn't
supposed to be like this.
I know I can't base my life off of others, but sometimes I'm
sick of waiting and life keeps giving me the slip
Time keeps escaping from me and my mind is racing,
fumbling on my missed opportunities

Once more I ask for an encore on the clock
Just another day to restart.
Life gets tough but in the end, I'm glad that I'm not at square
one again.

Give me a reason to live...Give me a reason to care... I go
through so many things it leaves my mind impaired

Maybe the reason I love so hard is because I just want some
back
I think I deserve it...love
Sometimes I just want to feel worth it...
I'm working on myself to be self-sufficient but it's hard.

Help

Here is my muffled scream two octaves below a yelp
This is my cry for help
My fear of asking for assistance
Scared of the persistent thoughts in my brain and oh how
they cause me pain

When things are unique, bright, and beautiful in my life:
I never write about them
I feel stuck...
Am I trying to hold on to what color is left in my world?

I feel like I'm on a downwards spiral, a swirl
It feels like an anchor on my brain, weighing me down,
making me ashamed.

The only reason I'm gaining weight is because
I keep take, take, taking other people's stress in
And it keeps break, break, breaking my body

and I feel like I have depression...

Most things I write are filled with sorrow, but me trying to
get it out, is my way of making it to tomorrow

And no... I would never do it. I have too many people I care
about who rely on me and would be crushed... if I would...

but sometimes I think about it.

I keep healing from shit and life keeps reopening the wounds

I try not to break in front of people.
In private I pick up the pieces, the ones that nobody sees and
I'm scared of developing a disease because of how
My stress,
depression,
and anxiety
sink in deep.

As I look into the sky (honestly, it's just my ceiling) and
pretend I don't know any emotions I'm feeling, my gut starts
twisting about:

Always thinking about others and never herself.

What did this stem from? What could it be?
Thinking back, was anything ever secure?
Or were my eyes just too pure to see the nasty, gritty realities
before me?

I turn off the noise and my ears are ringing, it's difficult to sit
in this feeling.

I'm putting this entry to a close
but I know I'll get better,
I just hope it's sooner than I know.

Reflection

Mirror mirror on the wall, who's the fairest of them all?
Well not me.
As I'm crying in the bathroom and letting out my steam,
I cannot see the slightest bit of glee, from my eyes.

An argument in my head.
A battle for dominance as I'm trying to be more positive.
I feel like I've hit rock bottom but not quite as I've seen the
bottom before
I feel as though I'm hanging off a ledge swinging back and
forth and struggling to climb.

I feel like I can't see the sunrise to my rainy skies, and I
question God, why?
Why am I stuck in my head?
It feels like a battleground and every failure is a pushback to
my positivity

I feel like the thoughts in my head are getting stronger and
I'm scared
Scared of my reactions...
Scared of my anger,
my depression,
my sadness....

I feel like I have to hold back for everyone
My frustrations make me want to shout but I have to...
no... need to
be quiet as a mouse because they'll fear me, they'll lose respect
for me
or at least that's what my thoughts in my head keep telling
me.

I just want to be me without teetering between loving and
hating myself
and placing my worth in my grades.

One day I'm up
another, I'm down.
When I don't have my go-to people to rant to, I feel like an
utter clown.
I feel defeated and most don't see it.
They think I'm self-sufficient when I feel nothing but
emotionally deficient

Sorry for myself....

I feel like I want help, but I don't trust people here and not
everyone is able to lend me their ear for my situations

Am I worthy of love?
Sometimes my head makes it hard to believe so
Because I put my feelings down to cater to others, hold my
tongue to be thoughtful and not hurt people but everyone

doesn't think the same...
My mind and heart go under a flame in my burning desire for
my future, but I feel pain in people not understanding me,
helping me, taking weight off my shoulders.

I think my love language is acts of service because under the
surface I wish people did half as much for me as I do for
them.
I'm always "oh so understanding" of people's situations and
try my best to help wherever I can, and I wish I can meet
someone the same as I am.
And no, I won't be looking for this in a man because this is
a burden that's in my hands and something I should do for
myself.

How do I be unapologetically me and feel free and release
myself from these chains of servitude?
How do I communicate what I'm feeling to others? The
answer seemed so obvious a few years ago...

Little miss problem solver, little miss therapist how will you
get yourself out of this?

Liberation

I feel as though I'm looking into a mirror
As a Black American this sight looks all too familiar
Hearing our screams and pleas, just asking for the slightest bit
of compassion, of humanity...

Yet it feels like our cries fall on deaf ears
For those who are in power don't care, as our bodies drop,
their wallets get stuffed

Profit off our labor, our pent-up anger, our existence
Then kill us when we try to create a resistance
They think we will lay over and die but we are roaring and
alive
And I know my God will punish you, the wicked will never
survive

New Beginnings

Being alone doesn't seem too bad.
After taking the time to myself, I'm actually quite glad.
I'm out of my head and into reality.
I spent time healing

When I decided to take a break, many people called me brave
while some, even though they didn't outright say it: thought
that I was stupid...
What if I don't come back?
If I switch up now: what will I do?

That's what I'll figure out
I realize that life has many opportunities and I'm still young.
I have hope for the future.
It took me so long to say it, but I finally feel... happy.
My unrequited love turned out to be a dick, but I'm elated
that
I didn't just sit and wait for him to come back.
If I kept waiting on him and wagged my tail like a puppy, I
would still be in misery

Acceptance

Now it's time to work on me. I realize that being alone
doesn't necessarily mean being lonely.
This time I'll look at my shadow and step into it instead of
being scared.
My shadow is me. I can't keep fleeing myself. I can't escape, so
I got to know her.
I Got to love her.
Cherish her.
Give her all that she wanted.

Back then I always looked into other ways of making her feel
better like helping other people or doing good deeds when in
reality, all she needed was
me & God,
A little bit of elbow grease and we got along.

I was running away from her for so long, but now we're
running away in-this race called life together.

V

When it rains it pours

How do I describe this

I feel so out of body, like I can see me in every different angle,
Everytime, I think of you....
Nah I'm giving you too much credit
Everytime, I think of the world. Things outside of myself I
start to ponder

Who am I, what am I here for... I mean I have an idea
Life is just so strange; I don't want to give my soul in
exchange for wealth or fame
Giving it to God has been a blessing
However, part of me feels like I'm regressing
I'm scared of change, but I keep running towards it
Failure, excuses and the thoughts that remain are all I know
It's hard to let that go...
I healed my trauma so there's nothing to hold me back
But I'm scared of that...

What?
What are you scared of?

I have nothing to excuse me
Seeing what's going on in the world right now makes me
realize I have nothing to lose
But I'm paralyzed
Paralyzed on the path to success because... I don't know
I'm afraid of the responsibility that will come next

What happens when I achieve this greatness?
I'm always expected to succeed,
but I've always known in my heart that it's easier to lay down
and grieve

Grieve what?

Anything and everything
I fear that I may be too ambitious
Although I'm surrounded by potential and greatness,
there's always the shadow of my past pulling me down

But I thought you healed

I did! I did!
I think I did....
I mean
I'm self-analyzing and critical
Sometimes even cynical of myself and situations
It took some time, but I was able to break out of my sadness
I pulled myself out of the pit of pity
Nursed myself to health
Cried out to God, he heard my shouts
I embraced him
United again
Time and time again I've fallen and picked myself up again,
I'm just scared for the time I won't be able to get back up

Wake up
What's missing?

I don't know there's something that feels hollow
I don't exactly feel sorrow or emptiness
I feel like if I stand here, I'm complacent
Contributing into the mess of the world if I don't try to clean
it up
I can't....no I won't just stand stiff even though the thoughts
that echo through my mind try to hold me still

Who are you?

Motivational purgatory

I hate being stagnant
No lie, I'm in this emotional limbo
Motivational purgatory as I'd like to call it
Everything feels on fire but at the same time it's not
Should I stop, drop, and roll or be engulfed by the flames of
life?
...Washed over with a wave of anxiety

Sometimes it's easy to to sink back into these feelings
It's difficult to go against the grain
In the moment it feels as though sadness is all I've ever known
That loneliness has nursed me, rocked me to sleep, comforted
me

It's scary that I've grown
Grown from the nuclear family of feelings that raised me and
made me who I came to be
Motivational purgatory has me questioning if I'm made to be
who others say I'm meant to be

Sorry to break your expectations
But self-sabotage keeps calling me and his words sound
enticing
And to add the icing on the cake my fear of failure won't
allow me to seek it because everyone believes in me

I feel overwhelmed
In over my head
My tough bravado finally slipping
I felt happy, but what's missing?

I just wish that I couldn't think for a minute
Be mindless
That someone can take over this ship
But I have to stick to my plan and keep going

College makes it hard to process
Just a continuous cycle of feelings, just stirring
I miss my friends
I miss my family
I just want to sit there and rot

But I can't ....
Can't mourn the girl I used to be
Can't sit in this feeling
Can't stay here too long, I need to get up and move on...

I want to live

Finally, I'm at a place in life where I don't want to passively
die
I don't want to stand idly by while life passes me
I don't want to stay miserable

I want to live
Everything is finally screaming inside me
In my soul, something is roaring
My heart is pounding
Pumping my blood, my essence through my body
My lungs, I'm finally allowing myself to breathe

But I'm scared
I don't know why
Why I get so fixated on death
Maybe it's because of my family and friend who left this plane
of existence
Only to become just a memory

I don't want that to be me
Even though that will happen eventually

Sometimes I'm fixated on when
When it'll happen
What will I feel?

Will I be happy that I'm going with God?
What will my family and friends think when I'm gone?

I don't know
Why am I assuming I'll go before everyone else?
Is it because that happened to them? Those family members
and my friend?
It's just...
I'm afraid

I wanna live so bad it hurts

Candy gram girl

Every year I'd sit idly by, waiting for the possibility of
receiving a candy gram
So excited for the thought that somebody liked me
That someone would show their affection to someone like me
through a simple Loli

Seeing all the girls smiling, receiving theirs. I was happy for
them.
Maybe next year I'd thought
Still hopeful

Then year after year
I remained candy-less
Not one?
What was so wrong with me that I couldn't receive one treat?
The reality was all too bittersweet

For just once I wanted to be someone's candy gram girl
I could give them the world ...

Maybe this isn't about candy...
Maybe it's about being chosen

And although I chose me, pretty recently compared to my
candy gram days

I still hope and can't wait for my future partner to love me the same...

Maybe he's a candy gram guy... Waiting for his chance as I did with mine

Bear with me

My baby
My sweet future lover
Please bear with me...
I want to do and experience so much with you, but please
bear with me

I want you to kiss me 10,000 times
Even though I'm so squeamish
I want to hold hands and be lovey with you
Whisper sweet nothings to you
Even though I'm scared...

My sweet lover, please
Bear with me...

Standing in the Rain

Sometimes I wonder
Does God ever weep for me?
Walking in the rain gives me a feeling that's hard to explain
Tranquil yet... Disgusted at the muck that this downpour has
constructed
I like rain from afar
I like the beauty it brings

My child-like wonder was strong and chaotic like lightning
and thunder
Now I grieve at the thought of how fast it has gone
And I sit here and ponder does God weep for me?
Does a strong wind and rain indicate his pain?
His cry for me
Sometimes it's hard to believe how many chances I've been
given

As I stand here
The rain isn't quite bad

Afterword

A Letter to the Reader:

Dear Reader,

I started writing this book when I was 15. It didn't start off as a book, they were just poetry 'do nows' that I had to complete in English class. I was just a kid who liked art but couldn't find any other way to articulate the complexities of my teen life. When I started writing poems I finally felt as if I was naturally good at something. (My parents were both songwriters and I was always disappointed that I never picked that up from them.)

Ever since I was 14, my mom told me "Hurry up and write a book so we can be rich already!" I rolled my eyes and ignored her because I'd never thought I could do it. I was just a sad kid with many emotions bottled up under the surface that many couldn't see.

Because I was the "good kid" with "good grades" I was left alone. Alone with all these thoughts and nowhere to put them except to the paper, since I couldn't draw it out. If you have a kid or know a kid or heck an adult, who seems to be fine, please check up on them. I didn't think I'd make it past 13, but here I am with my book, hoping that this helps at least 1 person.

This is dedicated to them & kid me, who thought no one could hear them, who wished someone looked deeper into the words they spoke, who needed to hear that they were loved and needed, and they'd make it.

My dear reader, I hope you check in with yourself, your friends, family, co-workers, community members, etc. after this. It is so important that you check in with yourself and those around you now more than ever. I love you & Jesus loves you too.

- XOXO
 Jelyse Williams (the coolest author in the world)

It's okay to ask for help!

The content of this book is heavy, so I would like to provide you with resources in case you or someone you know needs support.

Suicide and Crisis Lifeline: 988 or Lifeline Chat

Crisis Text Line: Text HOME to 741741

National Domestic Violence Hotline: (800) 799-7233

Childhelp National Child Abuse Hotline: (800) 422-4453

Darkness to Light Child Sexual Abuse National Helpline: (866) 367-5444

RAINN National Sexual Assault Hotline: (800) 656-4673

National Eating Disorders Association (NEDA) Helpline: (800) 931-2237

National Mental Health Hotline: (866) 903-3787

Substance Abuse and Mental Health Services Administration (SAMHSA) National Helpline: (800) 662-HELP (4357)

About the author

Jelyse Williams is known as the girl with 101 hobbies! From poetry to boxing she does it all. Her poetry book is one of the first projects she's ever pursued in writing. As an anime & cartoon enthusiast, she hopes to expand into writing/illustrating fiction books in the future! She will certainly keep you on your toes for whatever is next.

Follow her on social media to hear more about her upcoming projects & her other silly shenanigans:

Instagram: @_jelyse_
Art Instagram: @jjmoon_is_boss
YouTube: The Bonnet Bandit
TikTok: @jjmoon_is_boss